The laws of the BetaCodex

Niels Pflaeging I Silke Hermann

BetaCodex Press

Imprint
The laws of the BetaCodex
1st edition, 2023
© 2023 by Niels Pflaeging, Silke Hermann
contact@betacodexpress.com

BetaCodex Press – a Red42 brand
Matthias-Claudius-Strasse 16
65185 Wiesbaden, Germany

Concept & design: Niels Pflaeging
Illustration: Pia Steinmann, pia-steinmann.de
Translation: Rijon Erickson, Niels Pflaeging, Matt Moersch

ISBN print book: 978-3-948471-26-2
ISBN Ebook: 978-3-948471-27-9

For questions, suggestions, inquiries & further information:
contact@betacodexpress.com.
Visit us online: betacodexpress.com, redforty2.com

Introduction

This booklet is intended to give you, dear reader, condensed insights into the character and the inner workings of the twelve principles of the BetaCodex – in a concise, yet comprehensive form!

Again and again, we have been asked what exactly needs to be done to bring the individual principles of the BetaCodex to life in an organization. In this brochure, you will find distinctions and tools that will help you not only to grasp the respective Beta principles in its meaning, but also to fill those principles with meaning, in the context of your own organization.

The challenge of Beta, however, goes beyond the question of understanding individual laws or principles. The BetaCodex is expressly not intended as a "menu", from which you may choose as you wish! Rather, all the twelve principles reinforce each other: Together, they outline a consistent, indivisible system of organizational governance. So the quest for Beta is not really about any individual principle or law – it is about the connections between them!

In this booklet, we compare all Beta principles with their respective, opposite Alpha principles. This should serve to clarify context and make the principles less abstract. As a whole, the Alpha principles form another self-contained, coherent system. To those of you who want to take responsibility for designing the system in your organizations, we recommend you opt for one single system – Alpha or Beta! We advise you to use the Beta principles as the only viable option in an age of complexity, of course. Mixing the two models will inevitably lead to unsatisfactory, hardly sustainable results. You can't be a little pregnant. Coherence is key!

The "BetaCodex Clock" exercise at the end of the booklet offers a great way to figure out and to discuss crucial connections in your own organization.

We hope you will enjoy reading this booklet as well as thinking & acting in Beta!

§1 Team autonomy. Connectedness with purpose, not dependency

If an organization is to become faster, more flexible and more robust, it must align its teams with clients and the market – rather than with hierarchy, bosses and 'the top'. To give teams freedom and responsibility to think & act makes sense. We call that leadership. An organization that allows itself to be led in such a market-oriented fashion will reap success.

In Alpha

Command and control –
lines of control and dependency

The world is complicated –
formal and dead organizations are sufficient
and appropriate

The world is controllable –
a static world view

Repetition dominates –
automation and standardization as answers

Make & sell, stockpile production
and push product into the market –
'push'-business models with intermediaries

Tayloristic thinking –
separation between thinking and doing

Humans are seen through the
lens of "Theory X" –
as lazy and deficient

People must be forced
to perform and to do the work

Organizations need to motivate people –
through rewards, punishment and bribes

Activities and actions of people are controlled –
they must abide by rules and regulations

Methods and tools are prioritized –
individual knowledge & capability
are bottlenecks

The patriarchal impulse of managers
reigns supreme

In Beta

Sense and respond –
Connectedness to purpose and empowerment
of teams

The world is complex –
in addition to the formal, organizations need to
be informal and alive

Everything is in flux, nothing stands still –
an evolutionary world view

Surprise dominates – responsibility
and team empowerment as answers

Just-in-time;
sell first, then produce –
"pull' business models, direct sales

Systemic thinking –
integration of thinking and doing

Humans are all "Theory Y",
there are no "Xers" – people are intrinsically
motivated and filled with potential

If you give people a challenge and space for
development, they will make an effort

The work itself is motivating –
people are motivated through opportunities
to perform and learn

Work the context & cultivate principles –
trust that people can draw conclusions and
make smart decisions, based on principles

Ideas and theory are prioritized –
collective potential is unlimited
and learning is endless

The entrepreneurial impulse of all members
of the organization reigns supreme

§2 Federalization. Integration into cells, not division into silos

A decentralized network organization consists of many small, functionally integrated, self-organized and market-driven teams, each of which are responsible for their own results. Alpha organizations have no chance of competing against this type of cell structure network. When markets become complex, decentralization always wins.

In Alpha

Relationships are based on power
being exercised from top to bottom –
with pushing or pressure from bosses

Hierarchical structure, bureaucracy –
formal power and lines of command

Hierarchy embodies power – internal
references – management versus employees

The org chart is the organization –
Informal Structure is suppressed

Work must be controlled by hierarchy –
principle of external control

Functions, divisions, departments, staff units,
cost centers – dependent areas

Functional division creates the structure –
departments contain few and similar roles

Cross-functional work requires interfaces
and process management

Managed client proximity and relationships,
key accounting, divisions,
sales control and steering

The sales area sells –
sales people are responsible for revenues

For newly emerging tasks and problems,
create new, fixed departments and jobs

The best leaders have the widest
span of control – employees are never perfect

Functional divisions, product dominance
or matrix structures dominate
the organizational design

Functional division and deep specialization
are highly efficient

In Beta

Relationships are based predominantly on value
creation, with steering from the outside
towards the inside – 'market pull'

Network structure, entrepreneurship –
informal networks and flows of value creation

Market embodies power –
external references – periphery and center

The network is the organization –
Value Creation Structure and Formal Structure
are largely identical

Work is controlled by teams themselves –
principle of self-control/learning/improvement

Network cells as mini-companies within
the company – interdependent units

Functional integration creates the structure –
cells contain many and highly diverse roles

All value-creation is inherently cross-functional –
functional separation must be avoided

Decentralized business teams make decisions
about clients themselves,
steer themselves while seeing their results

Business cells in the periphery
run the business – everybody sells!

Almost everything can be done by volunteers
and by temporary task forces

Teams will always be limited
to 4 to 8 people – teams can be "perfect"

Functional division, product dominance and
matrix organization all contradict the primacy
of decentralization

Functional integration is more fun, and allows
people to develop mastery all the time

§3 Leaderships. Self-organization, not management

Leadership and self-organization are not just related – they are the same! Leadership arises in the space between humans, in three varieties, within the three structures of an organization. This requires elimination of management as division between thinkers and doers, and absence of internal steering. Self-organization intensifies where "performing-with-each-other-for-each-other" and team-based autonomy fully unfold.

In Alpha

Managers steer the work —
every team needs a boss

Hierarchy leads to stability
and is visible everywhere —
Pressure through power steers

Bosses are the only visionaries —
they rule by command and control

Managers keep the place running —
they take care of operational efficiency

Leadership is something for a few —
it happens at the top

Leadership is linked to position,
it happens at headquarters, especially —
it is an art that requires leaders

Companies need strong managers who
demand, accuse, assign blame

Authority arises from position
and status symbols

When problems happen: Search for culprits —
activism, "passing the buck"

Problems are solved with new methods
and tools — consultants and management
methods are important

Ideally, you have a strong,
powerful human resources (HR) department

Planned, or managed change — managers
decide about changes to be made, early-on

Solutions are developed behind closed doors
first, then convincing & enforcement begins,
force is applied when necessary

In Beta

The market steers the work already —
managers are superfluous for value creation
and often obstructive

Hierarchy is trivial (everyone has a boss),
but for the work, hierarchy does not matter —
market pull leads

Everyone has vision and is important —
having bosses is undesirable

Managers serve those who do the work —
leadership is working the system, together

All are involved in leaderships or leading —
Leadership is widely distributed and ubiquitous

Leadership exists in the center of the organization and at its periphery — it is a dynamic
that arises in the space between all actors

Companies need strong principles — adherence
with standards can be demanded by everyone

Authority arises from reputation/mastery, skill,
recognition/attribution, experience, attitude

When problems happen: Ask 'why?' 5 times in
a row — work the system, develop/apply theory

Problems can only be solved with better thinking and by working the system — Our people
can think for themselves, thank you very much!

Ideally, you do not have a human resources
department — outsource what's needed, or the
thing is done by all

Systemic, complex change — those involved in
change work decide as late as possible

Make urgency perceivable first, invite everyone,
then develop solutions together with
all the willing

§4 All-around success. Comprehensive fitness, not mono-maximization

An organization should always grow in such a way that it can survive in the long term. Size is unimportant. Growth is not a goal, but usually just a type of problem to factor into what you value. Do not put your organization in a situation in which it only survives if it grows. Never confuse sales, profits, size, or market share with success.

In Alpha

Success means achieving self-defined,
set goals – 'we set ourselves ambitious goals'

The business of business is making money –
financial results are the purpose
of an organization

There is natural, eternal conflict
between the stakeholders

Customers come 1st –
when in doubt, maximize shareholder value

Grow aggressively in good times
to take advantage of economies of scale

The little ones are eaten by the big ones

Size is important – more is always better

Size and market power are top goals –
be big! – have the highest market share

Overconfidence due to self-induced
market blindness, inward focused,
preoccupation with oneself

Company acquisitions and mergers
serve the ego of managers

Layoffs are inevitable in crisis
and they are a management task

In times of boom you can put on fat –
cyclical behavior, overeating followed by diet

Always look good in the public eye,
display executives as heroes –
at the expense of other stakeholders

In Beta

Success will always mean winning against the
competition – everything else is navel-gazing

The business of business is people –
making money is not the purpose, but a pre-
condition of doing business/staying in business

There is a positive, virtuous cycle
between the stakeholder groups

Customers come 2nd, members of the organization come 1st – profit is a natural consequence of good work & a result of succeeding

Grow modestly in good times –
most economies of scale are a mere myth

Those which are comparatively less profitable
will be eaten up, or will just fade away

Quality & profitability above average are key,
size is pretty unimportant

Size is a problem, growth must never be the
goal – be agile! – have best quality & best cost

Humility through transparency,
constant market focus, avoidance of wishful
thinking, a keen eye for complacency

Mergers destabilize organizational models
and culture. Keep managers' egos in check

Layoffs are the ultimate admission
of systemic mismanagement

Resource discipline both in boom and in crisis –
healthy ways of action are ongoing topics –
"be boring but sustainable"

Never inhibit the flow between
stakeholder groups –
keep the virtuous cycle between them intact

§5 Transparency. Flow intelligence, not power obstruction

In Beta, transparency is mandatory: numbers, figures, facts must be easily and quickly accessible to all teams and all members of the organization. Barriers to information trigger blindness and powerlessness in the uninformed. For the benefit of everyone's entrepreneurial ability to act, Beta requires renouncement of information power.

In Alpha

Status and power through information –
information is held by few

Information systems are closed –
employees are untrustworthy

Transparency leads to loss of control
and may provoke unethical behavior

Everything is confidential –
open information systems are unthinkable

Internal transparency is risky –
the dependency that arises from a lack of transparency is a necessary evil

Information will overwhelm people –
the truth is dangerous

Special reports and ad hoc reports
as a tool for executive micro-management

Lengthy, controlled distribution of information –
costly reporting systems

Salaries and compensation are kept secret –
employees will interpret differences in salaries
as injustice

Data is processed for different purposes & recipi-
ents, and polished/sugarcoated as needed

Customers and suppliers are contractually
bound – secrecy

Knowledge is managed – information systems
are designed to hoard knowledge and for
surveillance of employees

In Beta

Empowerment through information –
information serves all

Information systems and books are open –
employees are trustworthy

Transparency is an ideal mechanism of control,
it prevents nepotism, corruption, theft,
manipulation

Very little is confidential –
open information systems save a lot of money

Transparency is the basis and a necessary pre-
condition for entrepreneurial thinking

Information is to the brain what oxygen is for
the human body – information overload is a
myth, the truth is bearable

Open books elevate economic consciousness
in all – the business side of work becomes
observable

Everyone sees the same information,
at the same time – freely supplied

Information on salaries and compensation can
be visible to all – people find salary differences
quite natural

There is a uniform view of the data for all, plus
free access – dressing-up data is frowned upon

Customers & suppliers are bound by trust
and cooperation – having maximum access to
information systems

Knowledge cannot be managed – information
systems must support networked collaboration
and bolstering of informal structure

§6 Market orientation. Relative Targets, not top-down prescription

Beta requires a few, simple, long-running, self-adjusting goals. Teams compare their performance with their own past performance or externally, but always with figures that are "actuals". They interpret their own performance through actuals-to-actuals comparisons, not plan-to-actuals variances. Team-based self-control like this draws attention to permanent, continuous improvement.

In Alpha

Everything is measurable – measuring a lot is effective, and important for control purposes

Management by Numbers – rules, norms, values govern people's actions

Objectivity is achieved through measurement – What gets measured gets done

Fixed targets provide challenges – individual, negotiated targets/agreements and management by objectives enable this

Targets "produce" performance – without targets, no performance

Goals should be SMART – every goal is quantifiable

Measurement of performance versus fixed plans – with Plan-to-Actuals comparisons and appraisals

Management punishes deviations from plan – interventions and micro-management from above

Everything can be a target – from sales quotas, revenue and earnings, to sick leave rate and indicators

Targets are cascaded from top to bottom, broken down, derived from each other and scaled

Rankings/comparisons of individual employees and managers – rewards/punishment of those above/below

Benchmark data is hard to come by – we are unique and unequalled

Comparisons are not always accurate enough – accuracy is important to performance systems

In Beta

Few things are measurable – too much measurement hurts thinking and freedom to act

Improving value creation is the focus – guidance comes from shared principles and external comparisons

Objectivity in the numbers does not exist – complexity eludes measurement

Fixed targets promote mediocrity – in complexity, negotiations around targets are nonsensical, and a symptom of command & control

Targets may provoke awareness & indicate direction – but better performance can only arise from better methods and ways of working

Legitimate targets are always relative – targets for improvement cannot have fixed deadlines

Assessment of performance in context and with hindsight – measures look at longer periods of time, with Actuals-to-Actuals comparisons and dialogue

Teams are responsible for their own performance, without interventions from headquarters or managers

Few things should be targets – only a few "relative" indicators matter (e.g. cost/revenue); never compare absolute values

Businesses are not machines – goal cascading and cause-and-effect relationships are fiction

Ranking and comparisons between teams for sportsmanlike competition – without rewards or punishments

It's easy to get benchmark data – there's always relevant competition

In comparisons, accuracy is irrelevant – targets are separated from salaries and appraisal

§7 Conditional income. Participation, not incentives

Compensation systems in a Beta organization take three fundamental insights into account. First: individual salaries or employee's incomes are ultimately determined by the market. Secondly: In an organization there is no individual performance, or individual success – ever. Thirdly: Money does not motivate – ever.

In Alpha

Money needs to be a matter of importance for everyone – pay affects performance

Pay the position –
personnel areas manage position/salary ranges

Keep fixed salary as low as possible – use variable compensation as a lever to exert pressure

Many piecemeal salary systems,
with variable compensation only for the few,
and additional privileges for "those at the top"

Variable pay serves as an incentive –
always link targets and compensation

Motivation is extrinsic – people must
be motivated – incentives are necessary

Dangle the carrot and the donkey will run –
well-designed incentive systems make behavior controllable, this will lead to better outcome

Individual performance must be stimulated
by (individual) bonuses and incentives

Constant stimulus and incentivization,
pay for performance, meritocracy

Reward every behavior
that executives consider important

Personnel cost is managed and minimized –
keep salaries as low as possible

People are greedy,
executives/managers make use of that

Bonus systems are needed to attract
and retain top talent

In Beta

Nobody should constantly have to think about money, constantly – pay is a 'hygiene factor', not a motivator

Pay the person, pay people for who they are –
fundamentally, the market determines salaries

Make pay/salaries fair and appropriate, then do everything to get money off people's minds

One consistent pay system –
variable compensation for all via profit sharing

Variable pay serves "participation",
not behavioral control – always separate
targets and compensation

Motivation is intrinsic – people are already motivated – in the long term, incentives will always be harmful

People are intelligent: incentivized people will game any incentive system – never use compensation to control behavior

There is no such thing as individual performance – team/overall success can be acknowledged by providing everyone with a share

Profit-sharing and/or equity participation
through company shares or "virtual shares"

Base salary compensates for time & work –
rewards are manipulative and disrespectful

Employee income is a social contribution –
show pride in employees and their mastery

Self-interest is human, greed is spurred
by incentives – in the long term, any company
has exactly the people it deserves

Employees who are come for the money
will also leave for the money

§8 Presence of mind. Preparation, not planned economy

The future is a complex problem: You can neither predict, nor manage it; certainly not by planning ahead over longer, specified time intervals. A system can, however, be designed in a way that its parts, teams, and interactions will always act in a spirit of presence and awareness, instead of following orders or plans. This type of system will be ready for any possible future.

In Alpha

Thinking needs planning –
acting without prior planning is negligent

Plan as much as possible –
planning is ideal when dealing with the future

Planning is particularly effective when it
is integrated, frequent and participative

Planning is used to deal
with the imagined future

Strategic planning as an annual,
structured process

Always integrate strategy and planning!

Strategy is demanding, analytical,
and long-term –
some things are strategic, others operational

Forecasting and planning are the same –
predictions and intentions converge
in the future

It pays to spend a lot of time and effort
on planning and forecasting!

Planning, planning, planning –
fear of errors

Project management and planning,
milestones

Problems can be solved with tools,
blaming and punishment,
or hiring a consultant

Don't just sit there – do something!

In Beta

Planning cannibalizes thinking and dialogue,
it is superfluous or harmful, depending on the
situation – following plans is negligent

Companies do not require planning –
it is the wrong technology for the job when
dealing with an uncertain future

In a complex context, planning will inevitably
fail - varying participation, frequency, or scope
cannot fix that problem

Preparation allows to achieve superior competitive performance in every possible future

Strategy is superfluous if there is constant
reflection/thinking – and if it is clear to everyone what the boundaries of the business are

Strategy and planning are both harmful

If you have conscious, action-ready, dialog-
ready people, then strategy is superfluous –
everything is strategic

Forecasting can occasionally be necessary,
one needs little of it, though – planning
presupposes choosing, prognosis does not

Better to stay alert and stay on our toes –
better look out of the window
rather than into the future

Testing, prototyping, scrum, iterative project
work – intelligent mistakes foster learning

If the task is complex, then project management is superfluous/inadequate

To solve a systemic problem,
one has to understand that problem's
systemic root causes

Don't just do something – sit there!

§9 Rhythm.
Tempo & groove, not fiscal-year orientation

In complexity, organizations need to resonate with markets: They should "swing".
This allows market dynamics to be used as a competitive advantage. Beta organizations create
intelligent encapsulations, so that parts of the organization can create grooves for themselves
that are in sync with their value creation. That's the opposite of steering within
some sort of fiscal cadence.

In Alpha

Steering from above

Monthly/Annual cycle-based control
and performance rituals –
calendar-based rhythms

Linear approaches, milestones

All parts of the organization are subjected
to management/steering cycles

Rhythm and sequencing of work
depends on meeting cycles

Long deadlines –
thinking ahead covers perennial periods

What can we do in the period?

Dictatorship of the bean counters:
All functions have to follow calendar periods

It is smart to decide as early as possible –
decide everything in the planning period!

Capacity utilization is paramount –
imposition, central intervention, market-push –
micro-management ensures constant pressure

Plan and enforce,
market partners as enemies

Keep thinking scarce,
because thinking is expensive

Fast is key

Wheels must be spinning all the time!
Keep moving! – do as much as possible

Managers pressure employees
in such a way as to create performance

At the end of the period, we will reboot

In Beta

Steering is provided by external markets/clients

Value creation grooves according to
market needs – only financial accounting
follows calendar periods

Empirical process, sprints, feedback loops

Smart encapsulation allows subsystems to
follow their natural rhythms – they can swing!

Teams time-box their own work –
sequencing follows client orders or groove

Thinking ahead covers short, concise periods;
appropriate to the work's nature

Which duration is required? How much time do
we want to spend on this? Time-box everything

Groove principle:
Each team/function has its own, rolling rhythm

It is smart to decide as late as possible –
when it's time and "on demand"

Tempo-orientation – value creation "swings"
with demand – freedom from steering and
hierarchical interventions ensures flow

Exploitation of opportunities,
constant/attentive listening to the market

Create conditions where thinking
and reflection are both abundant,
because thinking is cheap and valuable

Being in the flow is key –
never interrupt the flow of value-creation!

Activism leads to double work, waste and slow-
down –maximize the amount of work not done

Everybody designs systems in such a way that
they can groove and value creation can emerge

There is always a next iteration

§10 Mastery-based decision. Consequence, not bureaucracy

In a Beta organization, decisions are made as decentralized as possible. Where the problem occurs, decisions are made. Decisions are not to be made by bosses, but by people with mastery in the realm of a particular problem. Application of organizational principles and consultative-individual decision-making ensure consistent action and clarity in all matters.

In Alpha

Centralized decision-making, "the top" decides –
 managers are paid to decide

Decision-making is separated from work –
democracy in the enterprise is impossible

Decision-making is a burden –
decisions are a top management duty

Bosses make better decisions than others –
centralized decision-making at the top
is fast, efficient and safe

Let the smartest person make the decision,
after some contemplation

Managers can make safe decisions –
if provided with good information

Decide as early as possible –
if possible, based on facts and hard numbers

Intuition is suspicious –
fact-based, rational decision making is best

Mistakes are bad –
Six Sigma and zero-defect initiatives

Implementation and execution
are always hard – people resist the wisdom
of management

Decisions should be made by the person
with the highest rank and the highest salary

Criticism is undesirable –
dissent is stupid

Many decisions are made in meetings –
but they often have no consequences

In Beta

Decentralized decision-making, outside/
periphery decides –all are paid to decide

Decision-making is integrated into the work –
democracy is the norm

Deciding is engaging/fun and a learning
opportunity – everyone should get to make
meaningful decisions at work

People with mastery make the best decisions –
centralized decision-making
is slow/expensive/demotivating/low-quality

Consultative individual decision-making
allows people with mastery to make the
highest-quality decisions

Decision-making in companies
is always entrepreneurial – and thereby risky

Decide as late as possible – those who decide
too early will be punished by reality

Intuition (unconscious knowledge)
is unavoidable in decision-making
and can be a powerful resource

Intelligent mistakes are necessary:
They offer learning opportunities –
continuous improvement is part of every job

The execution problem arises from the delay
between decision-making and action, and the
separation of thinking from doing

Decisions are made by those who are closest to
the problem and who keenly perceive urgency

Rejection of criticism is sabotage –
dissent prevents collective dumbing-down

Meetings serve to share information,
to disagree and to form opinions,
not to make decisions

§11 Resource discipline. Expedience, not status-orientation

In Beta organizations, financial resources officially belong to those who earn them: teams in the periphery. This creates consistency between "those who run the business" and "those who have the money". Resources are made available when they are needed, never earlier. Financial resources serve value creation, not status or ego.

In Alpha

Resources are always scarce
and therefore need to be managed

Keep the periphery under control –
headquarters are in charge

There are profit centers & cost centers ("over-
head") – which must be carefully managed,
or fixed costs will spin out of control

Planned resource management
and allocations – resources follow the org chart

Intense cost planning, cost management
and cost accounting

Cost cutting, budget cuts/control,
job cuts as executive tasks

Huge amount of performance indicators –
belief that numbers answer questions –
micro-management by leaders

Allocate resources centrally on a periodic basis,
where those who need resources are beggars –
allocation is optimized year after year

Accountants and accounting serves managers,
owners and external stakeholders –
speed is optional, closing the books every
month/year takes a lot of time

Investments require annual overall big-picture
planning – with intense negotiations around
investments and focus on numbers

Suggestion schemes & idea management –
a department or functional silo
is held responsible for innovation

In Beta

Land is usually meaningless, capital and funds
are not scarce – employee potential is the one,
unlimited resource to be boosted

Power to the periphery (e.g. branches),
cast out the center's arrogance

Money is earned in the periphery –
all cells have a profit & loss statement –
internal services are priced – Internal Markets

Team resources belong to the teams themselves,
and are made available when needed – allocations and budgets are unimportant

Costs cannot be managed – value creation can
be improved, waste must be fought –
cost accounting is usually worthless

Target costing, continually improving
value creation and fighting waste are
everyone's responsibility

A small number of indicators gives teams input
for reflection/thinking/learning, but no
answers – managers do not intervene

Decide on investments when they become
urgent – case-by-case decisions, not annually –
assess resource conflicts between projects
when they arise

Accounting serves teams, primarily –
speed of reporting is required for transparency –
fast, time-boxed monthly closing – external
reporting is a formality

Every good idea deserves start-up funding –
make decisions on investments as late
as possible

Open dialog on investment alternatives –
innovations emerge/may come from anywhere

§12 Flow coordination. Value-creation dynamics, not static allocations

Collaboration within an organization should be coordinated in a way that resembles market dynamics. In complexity, market-referenced self-control is more effective for coordination than planning cycles, processes, rules, and centralized steering. Centralized control destroys engagement, commitment, responsibility and effective collaboration.

In Alpha

Departments are linked through hierarchy –
functional coordination

Process management is important
to overcome functional/silo/area boundaries

Ever-growing central areas/overhead
(purchasing, engineering, marketing,
personnel, quality, auditing, etc.)
and interdepartmental interfaces

Push coordination from the top down –
"strategic central departments" sway power

Periodic, planned economic coordination –
annual agreements

Command/hierarchy dominates
during periods of fine-tuning and adjustment

Allocations and cost distributions, budgets,
allocated headcounts

Central departments, support functions, shared
services, business partners and centers of
excellence receive allocations from the center

Service Level Agreements,
centrally administered

Central areas have fixed/guaranteed
incomes or resources ("budgets")

Cost management, combined with allocations
("cost splitting") as a foundation
of centralized control

Standards (e.g. ISO) serve external/hierarchical
control of operations – follow procedures

In Beta

Links between cells: Value creation
flows from the inside-out, compensation for it
flows from the outside-in

In a networked Value Creation Structure,
processes turn trivial – cells/teams know no
other primacy than the flow of value creation

Dissolve central areas as much as possible,
by moving functions to the periphery and
by replacing them with temporary teams/task
forces – charge internal services to periphery

Pull coordination from the outside in –
resource pools or center hold no power –
all profit is made and retained in the periphery

Continuous market coordination
"as needed"

Internal markets, "pull"
and dialogue as dominant mechanisms

Internal markets and use-based service charges–
interplay of demand and supply

Business cells in the periphery have resource
responsibility and autonomy – central cells live
from services paid for by the periphery

Annual, half-yearly or quarterly negotiation
talks and agreements on services/prices

Central service providers must live with
fluctuations in demand, earn their living,
adapt to circumstances

Value flow/value creation
relationships as the foundation
of decentralized decision-making

Control is integrated into work – standards as
a means of team learning: they improve procedures further from a secured foundation

The BetaCodex clock

The laws of the BetaCodex are not an exercise in addition – they are an exercise in multiplication! The twelve principles form a consistent system. They influence and reinforce each other. However, the interdependencies between the individual principles are often less observable by the individual, depending on the context of the organization, depending on their own roles and personal viewpoints. It is worthwhile, thus, not only to reflect upon the content and the structure of the individual laws, but also with their relationships to each other, applied to their own organization.

This is how the exercise works:

On the following pages, the twelve principles of the BetaCodex are depicted in a representation that we call the "BetaCodex clock". This visualization makes it possible to depict relationships and reinforcements for your own organization.

You should start the following exercise on your own and then continue as a team!

1. Do this exercise alone first. Take about 30 minutes. Draw the connections between the principles with single effect arrows. Give each arrow a name: Try to name the nature of the connection as precisely as possible!

2. Compare your result with that of colleagues from your organization. Focus your conversation on the differences between your results – and what those differences mean for your organization and its evolution!

The BetaCodex clock

An exercise

12. Flow coordination
Value-creation dynamics,
not static allocations

1. Tear [Conr]
with
not d

11. Resource discipline
Expedience,
not status-orientation

10. Mastery-based decision
Consequence,
not bureaucracy

9. Rhythm
Tempo & groove,
not fiscal-year orientation

8. Presence of mind
Preparation,
not planned economy

7. Co
i
Part
not

onomy
dness
ose,
dency

2. Federalization
Integration
into cells,
not division
into silos

3. Leaderships
Self-organization,
not management

4. All-around success
Comprehensive fitness,
not mono-maximization

5. Transparency
Flow intelligence,
not power obstruction

6. Market orientation
Relative Targets,
not top-down prescription

onal
e
ion,
ives